Rich & Poor in
Ancient
Egypt

CLARE HIBBERT

FRANKLIN WATTS
LONDON•SYDNEY

First published in 2005 by
Franklin Watts
96 Leonard Street
London EC2A 4XD

Franklin Watts Australia
Level 17/207 Kent Street
Sydney
NSW 2000

Produced by Arcturus Publishing Ltd,
26/27 Bickels Yard, 151-153 Bermondsey Street, London SE1 3HA

© 2005 Arcturus Publishing

Series concept: Alex Woolf
Editor: Alex Woolf
Designer: Tim Mayer
Illustrator: Adam Hook
Picture researcher: Glass Onion Pictures

Picture Credits:
Art Archive: 4 (Egyptian Museum, Cairo / Dagli Orti), 6 (Egyptian Museum,
Cairo / Dagli Orti), 7 (Dagli Orti), 8 (Musée du Louvre, Paris / Dagli Orti), 9
(Ragab Papyrus Institute, Cairo / Dagli Orti), 11 (Musée du Louvre, Paris /
Dagli Orti), 12 (Egyptian Museum, Cairo / Dagli Orti [A]), 13 (Egyptian
Museum, Turin / Dagli Orti), 14 (Musée du Louvre, Paris / Dagli Orti), 15
(Carthage Museum / Dagli Orti [A]), 18 (Egyptian Museum, Cairo / Dagli Orti
[A]), 19 (Musée du Louvre, Paris / Dagli Orti), 20 (British Museum, London /
Jacqueline Hyde), 21 (British Museum, London / Dagli Orti [A]), 22 (Egyptian
Museum, Cairo / Dagli Orti), front cover and 24 (Dagli Orti), 25 (Musée du
Louvre, Paris / Dagli Orti), 28 (Pharaonic Village, Cairo / Dagli Orti), 29
(British Museum, London / Jacqueline Hyde).
Bridgeman Art Library: 27 (British Museum, London).
British Museum: 17

A CIP catalogue record for this book is available from the British Library.

ISBN 07496 5953 X

Printed in Singapore

* CONTENTS *

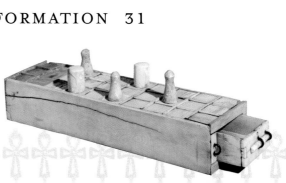

High Society

The richest person in ancient Egypt was the ruler, or pharaoh. Almost every pharaoh was a man, although there were a few female ones. The pharaoh ruled over the "Two Lands" of Upper and Lower Egypt and was thought to be a god on earth. He lived in the royal palace.

✖ NOBLES AND PRIESTS ✖

After the pharaoh and his family, the next layer of society was the nobility. Noblemen and women were wealthy landowners. The produce from their lands made them very rich and paid for a life of luxury.

The chief priests, who were in charge of the temples, were also rich.

Egypt's wealthy middle class was made up of scribes, architects, engineers and doctors. Highly skilled craftworkers, such as painters and jewellers, could also be very well-off.

Pharaoh Thutmose III reigned from 1479 to 1425 BCE. The cobra at the front of his headcloth is a sign of the sun god, Re.

THE KING OF EGYPT

Here is a description of the pharaoh: "He is Re [the sun god], by whose rays one sees, for he is one who illuminates the Two Lands more than the sun disk. He is one who makes [the land] green, even more than a high inundation: he has filled the Two Lands with victory and life."

From the Sehetepibre Stele (1900s BCE)

Low Life

Most people in Egypt were poor. Ordinary priests and craftworkers were not really poor, but they were certainly not rich. They worked hard and lived simply.

At the bottom of the heap were the enormous numbers of peasants and unskilled workers. They worked the fields to produce food for everyone, and built and maintained the kingdom. They put in long hours of back-breaking work and usually died young.

Life was not much better for the young men who worked in the army and navy as soldiers and sailors. Dancers, acrobats and servants had hard lives too.

❧ SLAVERY ❧

Some servants were slaves. Most slaves in ancient Egypt were foreign prisoners of war. Some slaves did really dangerous jobs, such as mining or quarrying out in the desert. Those who worked as domestic servants were the lucky ones.

A servant brings food. In his right hand he carries a pair of papyrus fans, which he will use to cool his master.

Mud Mansions

This model of a house dates to the 1300s or 1400s BCE. A row of decorative stone columns stands at one end of the garden.

Although the Egyptians used stone for their great temples and tombs, all houses were built from mud bricks — even the pharaoh's palace.

Inside a rich person's home, the walls were decorated with colourful paintings or inlaid with semi-precious stones. There was not much furniture, but it was beautifully carved. Beds often had wooden legs shaped like animals. There were tables, chairs and chests, some decorated with ebony and ivory.

✖ TOWN AND COUNTRY ✖

The pharaoh and nobility lived in cities, such as Memphis and Thebes. Most nobles lived in tall town houses with plenty of rooms. Some houses had a courtyard; all had a roof terrace with a canopy to keep off the sun.

Even for the rich, city life could be cramped. Many also owned a country estate where they could keep an eye on the harvest and had enough space for kitchen gardens and ponds.

Cramped Quarters

The poor lived in simple mud-brick houses within sprawling towns and villages. These were usually built on piles of rubbish or on top of the ruins of older houses. Inside, the house was divided into a few rooms, with areas for sleeping, eating and praying.

Kitchens were usually outside because of the risk of fire. In summer, many people chose to sleep on the cool, breezy roof, rather than inside the sun-baked house. Poor families had just a few, very plain items of furniture in their homes, including stools, headrests and storage chests.

◈ BARRACKS ◈

Special houses were built for the massive teams of labourers working on big projects such as temples, pyramids or tomb complexes. Their small, barracks-style housing units were really just a space to sleep. The workers ate together in a central canteen and probably washed down by the river.

Ruins of the huge housing complex at Deir el Medina. The builders and craftworkers who created the tombs in the Valley of the Kings lived here.

For Richer ...

Egyptians married young, usually to a partner chosen by their parents. In the richest families, couples often married within the same family — some pharaohs even married their sisters. The couple signed a marriage contract which gave each partner equal rights over any property.

The woman's job was to stay at home, run the household and raise the children. The mother chose her child's name. Children were breastfed for as long as three years, but rich women might pay a wet nurse to feed the child for them.

◆ CHILDCARE ◆

Children were very important, because when they grew up they could look after their parents and give them a proper burial. Most couples had five children, and people who could not have children often adopted.

Pharaoh Akhenaten affectionately holds hands with his wife, Nefertiti. Akhenaten ruled from 1352 to 1336 BCE.

... For Poorer

Egyptian women gave birth in an upright position. Here a mother kneels as a midwife delivers her baby. Other pictures show women using a low birthing stool for support.

Like the rich, the poor generally married within their own class. Most marriages were arranged, but some couples married for love. Poor people did not usually sign a marriage contract — partly because they could not afford to pay a scribe to draw one up, and partly because they did not own much property to share between them.

As in rich marriages, there was no official wedding ceremony. The marriage began when the bride and groom set up home together. However, even the poorest couples probably threw some sort of party to celebrate.

☙ GIVING BIRTH ☙

Some women had as many as fifteen children, but childbirth was a dangerous business. Roughly a third of babies died, and so did many mothers. Poor women could not afford to pay professional midwives. They usually gave birth at home, with a couple of neighbouring women there to help.

HOW TO TREAT A WIFE

The scribe Ani advises his son how to keep a happy household: "Do not control your wife in her house when you know she is efficient. Do not say to her 'Where is it?, Get it!', when she has put it in the right place. Let your eye observe in silence. Then you recognize her skill, it is joy when your hand is with her ..."

From *Instructions of Ani*

Colourful Collars

The rich wore finely woven linen, made into long, flowing dresses for women, and pleated kilts for the men. Sometimes men wore a woollen cape, too. Silk came late to Egypt, but the female pharaoh Cleopatra (51–30 BCE) wore silk dresses.

Clothes were bleached white, but people wore colourful beaded collars. The rich also liked gold jewellery set with semi-precious stones or faience (a kind of ceramic).

Wealthy women adorned themselves with colourful gemstones: blue lapis lazuli, purple amethyst, red carnelian and green feldspar.

A PRINCE'S GIFTS TO THE PHARAOH

"... armlets, gold bracelets, necklaces, collars inlaid with gemstones, amulets of every limb, garland crowns for the head, rings for the ears, every royal adornment.... All of these I have presented in the royal presence, and clothing of royal linen by the thousands, being all the best of my weaving workshop."

From the Piye Victory Stela

✖ HAIR AND MAKE-UP ✖

Both men and women rubbed scented oils into the skin and wore striking make-up. They used black kohl and green malachite for the eyes, as well as blushers and lipsticks.

Most people shaved their heads and wore wigs of plaited human hair. Boys – and some girls – kept one long lock of hair, known as the "sidelock of youth". Men stayed clean-shaven, but the pharaoh wore a ceremonial beard as a sign of kingship.

Coarse Cloth

The poor wore coarse, homespun linen. Linen came from the flax plant, one of Egypt's chief crops. The rough material was cut into simple loincloths for men, or dresses for the women. Women made the clothes, but men went down to the river to wash them — because of the danger of crocodiles! Servants wore finer clothes, given to them by their masters and mistresses.

∞ INEXPENSIVE JEWELS ∞

The poor liked jewellery and wore necklaces, earrings and rings made of shells or beaten copper. They rubbed cheap castor oil into the skin. It didn't smell wonderful but it kept the skin soft.

Many of the poor shaved their heads, just like the rich. This kept them cool and prevented headlice. Some women grew their hair to sell for wigs.

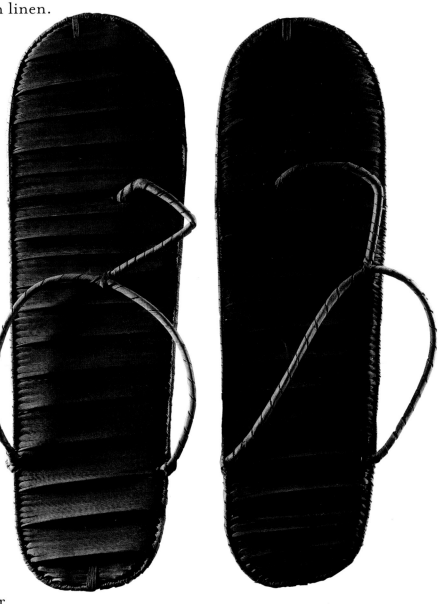

Most poor Egyptians went barefoot, but some servants wore simple sandals woven from papyrus reeds.

Fine Feasts

Meat was a luxury that only the rich could afford. They ate beef, mutton, goat, goose and duck. They also feasted on game animals, including antelope, ibex, gazelle, deer, ostrich and hare. Roast meats were served up at sumptuous banquets.

Many of the dishes were flavoured with expensive herbs and spices such as coriander, aniseed or cinnamon.

The rich also enjoyed lots of different cakes, biscuits and breads. The best bakers crafted dough into amazing shapes, even making cakes that looked like crocodiles!

❈ Garden Produce ❈

In the towns, the rich had small courtyard gardens where they grew fresh vegetables and fruit, including grapes. Some grapes were eaten dried as raisins, but most were used for making wine, which was fermented in special jars. Before drinking, the wine was sweetened with honey.

A husband and wife sit down to share a feast. The table is laden with meat and there is a drinking cup of wine for each of them.

Bread and Beer

Bread was the staple food, although making it was hard work. First, the wheat grains were ground and sieved many times to make the flour. This was made into a dough, then kneaded and baked. Sometimes the bread was flavoured with herbs or sweet, sticky dates.

The poor ate the same vegetables as the rich, including lettuce, cucumber, spinach, leeks and onions. People also ate fruits such as melons, figs, dates and pomegranates.

Most meals were washed down with beer, rather than water. It was made from soggy, half-cooked barley loaves, left to ferment in water.

This tomb model shows a kitchen. On the left, servants grind barley and knead bread dough. In the centre are barrels of fermenting beer.

⚜ GIFTS FROM THE RIVER ⚜

Beer and bread were gifts of the Nile, whose yearly flood spread rich mud over the fields and fertilized the crops. The river also supplied fish and small game birds such as cranes, quails and ducks.

TOO MUCH WINE

This is part of a story about Pharaoh Amasis (570–526 BCE): "Pharaoh drank an extremely large quantity of wine because of the craving that he had for a vat of Egyptian wine.... Morning came, and Pharaoh was unable to raise himself.... Pharaoh said: 'I have a terrible hangover. It isn't [in my] power to do any work at all.'"

From *The Tale of Amasis and the Skipper*

Costly Care

This 3,500-year-old fragment of papyrus contains instructions for making a medicine. The ingredients include honey, fat and galena (poisonous lead sulphide).

When they were sick, the rich visited doctors — and some of them *were* doctors! Medicine was such a well-respected profession that only people of high-born families could enter it. The very first physician, Imhotep (c. 2650 BCE), was later worshipped as the god of medicine.

Egyptian doctors trained at special schools, where they studied ancient medical texts. Medical students did not practise on real patients, but they were able to examine dead bodies.

✄ TREATING THE SICK ✄

Egyptian doctors used plants with healing properties, and spread honey, a known antiseptic, on open wounds. They also knew how to stitch up wounds, mend fractures and diagnose a pregnancy.

DOCTOR'S NOTES

These were jotted down around 1800 BCE:
"The patient ... feels a heavy, hot and inflamed body. He complains of being unable to tolerate his clothes and feels they do not warm him. He feels thirsty during the night. His saliva has the taste of unripe fruits. His muscles pain him as if he walked for a long distance."
From the Berlin Papyrus

Almost all doctors specialized in treating just one particular part of the body, such as the eyes, teeth or abdomen. The pharaoh had a whole army of court physicians, ready to treat his every ailment.

Homemade Healing

The very poor could not afford doctors. If they fell ill, they saved up to buy medicines from a chemist, or relied on homemade remedies. Most medicines contained herbs or other plant extracts. Thyme, for example, was taken for general pain relief, while dill relieved constipation.

⋖ COMMON COMPLAINTS ⋗

Disease spread quickly among the poor, because they lived so close together. There were outbreaks of malaria, smallpox, tuberculosis and cholera. People also suffered injuries at work, or developed lung diseases from breathing in too much sand.

With no doctors available to them, the poor turned to magic. They wore protective charms, or amulets, in the hope that they would stay healthy. The "eye of Horus", for example, was a stylized eye that kept watch for evil spirits.

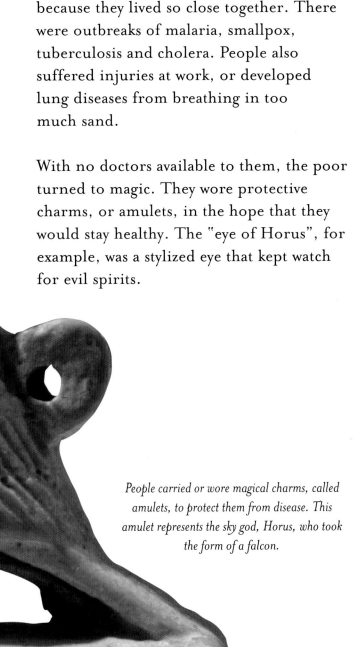

People carried or wore magical charms, called amulets, to protect them from disease. This amulet represents the sky god, Horus, who took the form of a falcon.

Privileged Pupils

Scribes were the best-educated ancient Egyptians. Boys who were going to become scribes began school at the age of five. They had to copy out rows of hieroglyphs and learn long passages of text off by heart.

Princes and princesses also learned reading, writing and maths, but they did not attend school. They studied with private tutors.

Scribes wrote on a kind of paper, made from papyrus reeds. Bundles of reed stems were tied together to make a paintbrush. This was dipped in ink made from soot or red earth.

✹ WORK AND PLAY ✹

Most well-off boys and girls did not have any schooling. Instead, their parents taught them how to manage an estate or run a household. Some boys did apprenticeships in order to follow a career such as medicine, architecture or the priesthood.

When they were not busy learning, rich children enjoyed activities such as swimming, riding and archery. They had toys, including rag dolls or wooden animals with moving parts. In the richest families, children kept pets — a cat, a dog or even a monkey.

ADVICE TO A YOUNG SCRIBE

"O scribe, do not be idle, do not be idle, or you shall be curbed straightway. Do not give your heart to pleasures, or you shall fail. Write with your hand, recite with your mouth, and converse with those more knowledgeable than you."

From the Papyrus Anastasi

Child Labour

Poor children did not need to read or write, and their parents could not afford to send them to school anyway. Both boys and girls were expected to help their parents and look after any younger brothers and sisters.

Most children learned to do their parents' jobs. Peasants' children took part in the sowing and harvesting. They even acted as human scarecrows to keep the birds off the crops! Servants' children ran errands or helped to prepare food. Sons of tomb builders were sometimes lucky enough to win a place on one of the building gangs, where they could do odd jobs and learn the skills of the craft.

These simple spinning tops were made of cheap, moulded quartz crystals. A child could start the top spinning by hand, or wind papyrus twine around it and then pull.

ᨒ FUN TIMES ᨒ

Not even poor children were expected to start work until they were five. Before then they played with simple toys such as balls and dolls, and made up exciting games, such as pretend battles.

Top Jobs

Everyone worked in ancient Egypt, even the pharaoh! Since he was thought to be a god on earth, it was very important that he took part in special ceremonies throughout the year. He also had to run the country, meet foreign officials and rule over his generals.

The best-paid jobs in the land were for high priests, officials and scribes. There were many official jobs in ancient Egypt, such as collecting taxes for the pharaoh or judging criminals. These jobs were almost always held by noblemen, although there were a few women scribes – and at least one woman judge.

✖ BEAUTIFUL THINGS ✖

Not all craftworkers were rich, but the most skilful ones were paid well for their work. They painted beautiful murals on the walls of temples and tombs, or designed stunning jewellery using semi-precious stones. Some of them made fine pottery; others carved elegant furniture.

Scribes were always in demand and earned good wages. They were employed to record court judgements or yields from the fields. This statue of a scribe dates to around 2400 BCE.

Tough Toil

This wall painting shows workers in the fields. They use curved knives called sickles to harvest the crop.

The poor did much more physical work than the rich. Hardest of all was *corvée*, or national service. This was when the pharaoh called on everyone in the land – except his officials – to work on a project, such as building a temple, farming some land or repairing an irrigation system. Richer people could buy their way out of doing national service, so in the end all the backbreaking work fell on the poor.

◁ HARD LABOUR ▷

By far the largest group of poor workers were the peasant labourers. The land that they cultivated usually belonged to the pharaoh, a temple or nobleman. Peasants worked long hours but earned scarcely enough to live on.

Another tough job was being in the army. Soldiers were expected to walk long distances on short rations and were beaten if they did not keep up.

A SOLDIER'S LIFE

"His rations and his water are upon his shoulder like the load of an ass, while his neck has been made a backbone like that of an ass. The vertebrae of his back are broken, while he drinks of foul water. He stops work [only] to keep watch."

From the Papyrus Anastasi

Rich Revels

The rich enjoyed throwing lavish banquets, and the pharaoh's feasts were the most extravagant of all. As well as eating and drinking, guests were entertained. Dancing girls performed acrobatic routines, including somersaults. Musicians played flutes, harps and cymbals.

❖ FAVOURITE PASTIMES ❖

In their spare time, Egyptian noblemen liked to go hunting with dogs, either at the marshy edges of the Nile or out in the desert. They used various weapons, including spears, arrows, throwing sticks and nets.

The board game of *senet* was popular with everyone in Egypt. The rich owned beautiful senet sets made of costly ebony and ivory, or inlaid with semi-precious stones.

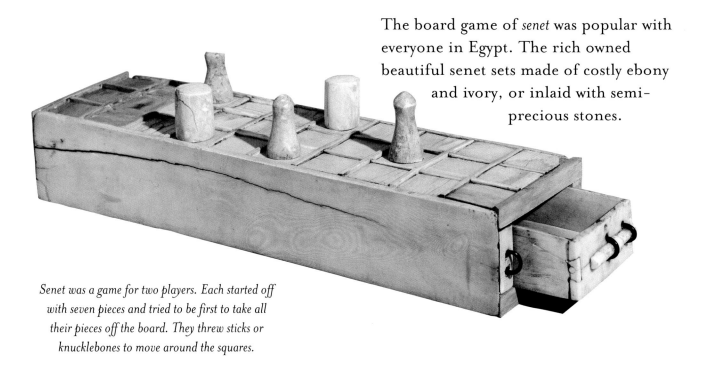

Senet was a game for two players. Each started off with seven pieces and tried to be first to take all their pieces off the board. They threw sticks or knucklebones to move around the squares.

HUNTING BY THE NILE

Bird-trapping and fishing in the marshes by the river:

"A happy day when we go down to the marsh, that we may snare birds and catch many fishes in the waters ... a happy day on which we give to everybody and the marsh goddess is propitious. We shall trap birds and shall light a brazier to Sobek [the crocodile god]."

From *The Pleasures of Fishing and Fowling*

Songs and Stories

Storytelling did not cost anything and was the main way that ordinary people relaxed in the evenings after work. Some stories recounted adventures of heroes, and myths about the gods, which sometimes explained natural events.

One tale, for example, told how the yearly flooding of the Nile came from the tears of the goddess Isis. She was said to be weeping to mark the anniversary of her husband Osiris's death.

☙ MUSIC AND DANCE ☙

The poor played simple percussion instruments, such as rhythm sticks and drums, to beat time while they worked. They also played music for relaxation. Love songs were popular, as well as ballads about heroes or pharaohs.

Not all dancing and making music was for pleasure. Poor dancers and musicians performed at funerals as professional mourners, as well as entertaining the rich at their banquets.

This wall painting from around 1350 BCE shows entertainers at a feast. The musicians have cones of perfumed grease on their heads.

Travelling in Style

On land, the very richest people used one-man horse-drawn chariots to move from place to place. Chariots were ideal for hunting trips or charging into battle, but horses were rare. Most rich people travelled in a litter, a chair on poles carried by servants.

✵ THE MIGHTY NILE ✵

All of the towns and cities in Egypt grew up along the banks of the River Nile, so people usually travelled by boat – it was much cooler! The rich had their own private boats made of reeds or wood. The finest ones, including the pharaoh's royal barge, were built of cedarwood, imported from Lebanon. Boats sailed south, because the wind always blew in that direction. When travelling north, they relied on a team of oarsmen.

Pharaoh Tutankhamun, who reigned from 1332 to 1322 BCE, rides into battle against the Syrians in a horse-drawn war chariot.
The scene decorates a wooden chest found in Tutankhamun's tomb.

Boats and Beasts

Even the poor travelled by boat. They built simple rafts or small fishing boats out of papyrus reeds. Unfortunately these did not offer much protection against the wild animals of the Nile – crocodiles and hippopotamuses!

There were also large passenger ferries and cargo barges. These ferried labourers and heavy supplies to the sites of the pyramids, tomb complexes or temples.

✤ LAND TRAVEL ✤

When on land, the poor walked. Some people wore reed sandals to protect their feet on hot or stony ground, but most went barefoot. They used sturdy cattle and donkeys to help carry supplies such as food or wine.

The poor also had to transport enormous weights, such as the 2.5-tonne stone blocks used to build the pyramids. It is likely that these were moved from the riverbank up to the building site using strong papyrus ropes – and the pulling-power of hundreds of men.

A LOVE SONG

"I am sailing downstream on the ferry, [Guided] by the hand of the helmsman, With my bundle of reeds on my shoulder. I am bound for [Memphis], And I shall say to Ptah [the creator], the Lord of Ma'at [universal order], 'Grant me my beloved this night.'"

From the Love Songs of Papyrus Harris 500

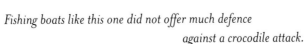

Fishing boats like this one did not offer much defence against a crocodile attack.

Sacred Secrets

The most important religious rites were performed by the pharaoh, or on his behalf by priests and priestesses. The pharaoh was thought to be the son of the sun god, Re. By carrying out special ceremonies, he helped to ensure a good harvest or the safety of his people.

A PHARAOH'S RELIGIOUS DUTIES

"Perform the monthly priestly service, don white sandals; Enrich the temple, be discreet concerning the mysteries; Enter into the holy place, eat bread in the house of the god; Replenish the offerings, multiply the sacrificial loaves; Increase the daily offerings …"
From the Teaching for King Merykara
(c. 2025–1700 BCE)

✖ HOUSES OF THE GODS ✖

Priests and priestesses also worshipped on behalf of the whole population. They chanted prayers and spells, made music using a sacred rattle called a sistrum and performed sacred dances. They also made daily offerings of food, wine and perfumed oils to the gods.

Priests and priestesses lived in the temple complexes built at Abydos, Thebes (Luxor) and nearby Karnak. Each temple was dedicated to a particular god, such as Re, Osiris (king of the dead), Thoth (god of knowledge) or Isis (goddess of love). Ordinary people were not allowed into the temples.

Ruins of the Temple of Amun at Karnak. Amun was originally associated only with the city of Thebes, but later became Egypt's supreme god.

Festivals and Shrines

Poor and rich alike gathered to watch the many religious festivals that took place throughout the year. During the festival of Opet, held at Thebes, they lined the banks of the Nile while statues of the gods were processed along the river.

People also visited small shrines where they could pray to a god and make offerings. If they could afford it, people paid to have their prayer engraved on to a small stone tablet called a stele. Some stelae included a picture of an ear, to make sure the god would hear the prayer!

⚜ HOUSEHOLD GODS ⚜

Most people had miniature shrines in their houses — small alcoves where they kept a statue of a god. Popular household deities included Taweret, the hippopotamus goddess of fertility and childbirth, and the dwarf god Bes, protector of households and bringer of domestic happiness.

Most Egyptian deities took animal form. Taweret, goddess of childbirth, was seen as a hippopotamus. Female hippos are known for fiercely defending their offspring.

Mummy Making

All ancient Egyptians believed that when they died they still needed their physical body for the afterlife. Rich people had their bodies preserved as mummies.

Mummification was a long, complicated process that took seventy days. Specially trained embalmers washed the body in scented oil and then carefully removed the organs – all except the heart. Next, they left the body in natron salt for forty days to dry it out.

❈ WRAPPING UP ❈

After packing the body with linen or sawdust and oiling the skin, the embalmers bandaged the mummy from head to toe. They slipped magic charms between the bandages. As they worked, a priest chanted special prayers and spells. He wore a mask of Anubis, the jackal-headed god of embalming.

Finally, a death mask was placed over the mummy's head and the body was placed in a wooden coffin and perhaps inside another box called a sarcophagus.

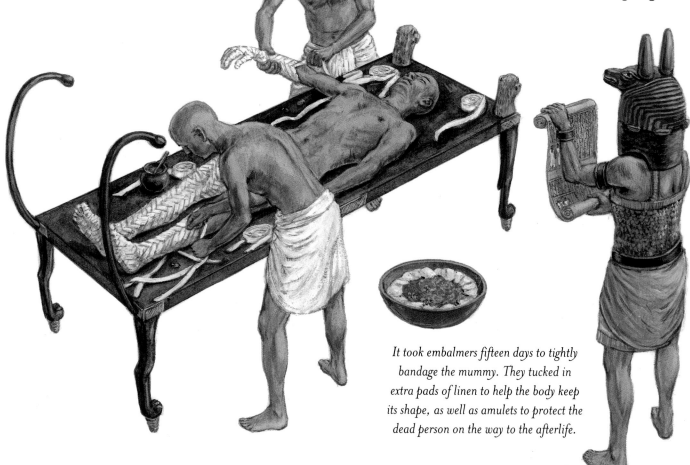

It took embalmers fifteen days to tightly bandage the mummy. They tucked in extra pads of linen to help the body keep its shape, as well as amulets to protect the dead person on the way to the afterlife.

Common Graves

The attention and skills of embalmers and priests were far too expensive for the poor, although there were a few exceptions. Servants were sometimes made into mummies so that they could be buried with their master or mistress, ready to serve them again in the next life!

✺ FUSS-FREE FUNERALS ✺

Most poor people were placed as they were in simple coffins made of papyrus reeds or, sometimes, wood. The very poorest were not even buried in coffins. They were simply thrown into shallow pits dug on the edge of the desert. Amazingly, these bodies were often brilliantly preserved. The dry desert sand mummified them naturally! Some poor people's bodies are even better preserved than the purpose-made mummies of the rich.

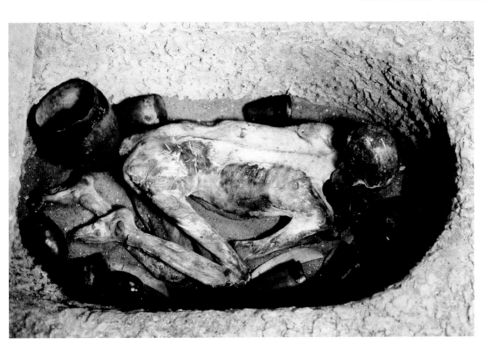

This man, buried with just a few possessions, was naturally preserved by the hot desert sand. Known as "Ginger", he lived around 3200 BCE, before Egypt was ruled by the pharaohs.

HOW TO MAKE A MUMMY

"First with the crooked iron tool they draw out the brain through the nostrils ... and after this with a sharp stone of Ethiopia they make a cut along the side and take out the whole contents of the belly, and when they have cleared out the cavity and cleansed it with palm-wine they cleanse it again with spices pounded up ..."

From Herodotus's *Histories*

Treasure-Filled Tombs

The mummified bodies of the rich were placed in a tomb, along with belongings for the afterlife. These included real clothing, jewels, furniture and weapons, as well as models of larger items such as boats and chariots. People were even buried with clay models of food and drink. Paintings on the wall showed the person's house and family, in the hope that the same riches and happiness would be enjoyed in the afterlife.

❈ TOMB TYPES ❈

The most spectacular ancient Egyptian tombs are the pyramids – towering triangular tombs built for some of the early pharaohs. The Great Pyramid at Giza was designed to help point the pharaoh up to the sky to join his father, the sun god.

Unfortunately, the pyramids were raided for the riches inside. Later pharaohs and other rich people were buried in hidden underground tombs, cut into the hard, desert rock.

One of the rooms inside Tutankhamun's tomb. Among the many treasures are three gilded wooden couches, shaped as a lion, a cow and a hippopotamus. At the far end, two statues guard the way into the main burial chamber.

Heavenly Hopes

Poor people didn't have specially built tombs, but they did make sure that they were buried with a few possessions and some food. Like the rich, they believed that their bodies would have to make a special journey to the afterlife, the heavenly kingdom ruled over by the god Osiris.

✍ JOURNEY TO OSIRIS'S KINGDOM ✍

First, the dead person had to ask a ferryman to carry him across a river. Then he had to go through seven carefully guarded gates. Atum, a creator god, and Hathor, the goddess of beauty, were there to help, but there were also evil gods, snakes and crocodiles to outwit.

HOW TO ENTER THE AFTERLIFE

"A man should say this spell when pure and clean, dressed in clothing, shod in white sandals, painted with black eye-paint, anointed with the finest myrrh-oil, and having offered fresh meat, fowl, incense, bread, beer and vegetables."

From the Book of the Dead

Next, the dead person had to face forty-two judges before his heart was weighed in the Hall of Two Truths. If the dead person's heart was heavier than the feather of truth, he was devoured by a monster. If his heart was light, he was allowed into the afterlife.

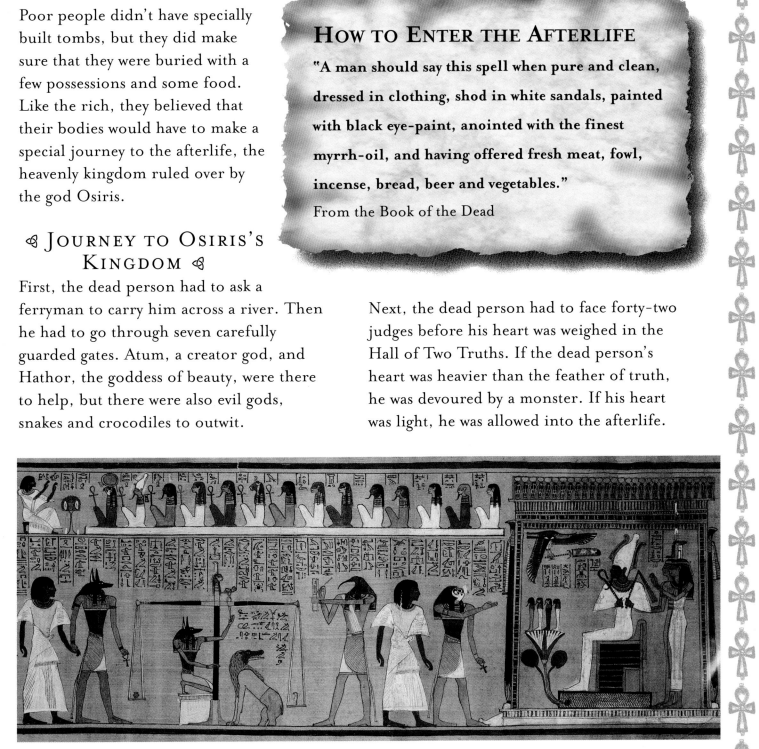

The god Anubis leads a dead person to the afterlife, then weighs his heart against the feather of truth. To the right, the god Osiris sits on his throne.

BCE

c. 7000 First farming settlements are established along the Nile.

4236 The first date in the ancient Egyptian calendar.

c. 3050 Upper and Lower Kingdoms of Egypt unite under one pharaoh, Narmer (Menes).

c. 3000 Hieroglyphic writing appears. City of Memphis is founded. Earliest mummy-making.

c. 2700 Trade for jewels and cedarwood begins with Lebanon, Byblos and Somalia.

c. 2650s Worship of Re (the sun god) begins. Step pyramids are built at Saqqara.

c. 2575–
c. 2465 Pyramids and Sphinx are built at Giza.

c. 1850 Egyptians conquer Nubia, to the south.

c. 1630 Asian invaders, the Hyksos, introduce the horse and chariot to Egypt.

c. 1550 Mummy-making process is perfected.

c. 1510 Construction of Temple of Amun-Re at Karnak.

1504 Death of Thutmose I, the first pharaoh to be buried in the Valley of the Kings.

c. 1500 The world's oldest-known medical text, the Ebers papyrus, is written.

c. 1380s Worship of Amun (a creator god) stops. Worship of the sun-disk god, Aten, begins. Capital moves to el-Amarna.

1330s The boy pharaoh, Tutankhamun, re-establishes worship of Amun. Royal court returns to Thebes and Memphis.

524–404 Persian kings rule over Egypt.

305–30 Greeks rule Egypt, following Alexander the Great's invasion. Capital moves to Alexandria.

30 Egypt becomes a province of ancient Rome.

Further Reading

The British Museum Illustrated Encyclopaedia of Ancient Egypt by Geraldine Harris and Delia Pemberton (British Museum Press, 1999)

The Story of the Nile by Anne Millard and illustrated by Steve Noon (Dorling Kindersley, 2003)

Kingfisher Knowledge: Mummies by John Malam (Kingfisher, 2003)

The Awesome Egyptians by Terry Deary (Scholastic Hippo, 1993)

CD-Roms, Videos, DVDs and Audiocassettes

Egypt — Secrets of the Pharaohs (National Geographic, 2002). Video and DVD.

Egyptian Gods and Pharaohs (BBC Audio Books, 2003). CD-Rom and audiocassette.

Websites

http://www.bbc.co.uk/history/ancient/egyptians/index.shtml

http://www.ancientegypt.co.uk/menu.html

http://www.ancient-egypt.org/

amulet A magical charm that protects the wearer.

anointed Rubbed with oil.

antiseptic Something that kills bacteria and prevents infection.

apprenticeship Working for someone in order to learn their trade.

balm A soothing ointment.

barracks Soldiers' living quarters.

brazier A small, contained fire.

cholera A usually fatal bacterial infection of the small intestine, caused by dirty water. Victims suffer diarrhoea, vomiting and cramps.

cultivated Describes land that is being used for growing crops.

diagnose Identify a condition or disease.

domestic Connected to a household.

embalmer Someone who treats dead bodies so that they do not rot away.

faience Coloured, glazed ceramic.

ferment Turn into alcohol through the action of yeasts.

fertility The ability to produce offspring or crops.

gazelle A small, wild antelope found in northern Africa and southwest Asia.

helmsman The person who steers a boat.

hieroglyph A small picture or symbol. The Egyptians wrote using hieroglyphs. Each hieroglyph might stand for a sound or a whole word.

ibex A wild mountain goat found in Europe, north Africa and Asia.

incense Resin, or plant sap, that gives off sweet-smelling fumes when it is burned.

inflamed Hot and swollen.

inundation Flood.

irrigation System of artificially watering crops, usually by transporting water to the fields from a river or lake along specially dug channels.

jackal A wild dog found in Africa and Asia.

kohl Black powder used as eye make-up.

loincloth A long piece of cloth that wraps between the legs and ties at the waist, worn as a basic garment or undergarment.

malachite A green mineral.

malaria A fever caused by a parasite of the *Anopheles* mosquito. It can be fatal.

mortgage Take out a loan of money, using one's house as security – that is, agreeing to hand over the house if the loan repayments cannot be met.

mural A wall painting.

myrrh-oil Highly prized, strong-smelling oil extracted from the bark of the Commiphora, or incense tree.

natron A natural rock salt, used by embalmers to dry out bodies.

papyrus A reed that grows by the Nile. The Egyptians used it to make all sorts of useful things, including ropes, baskets and a form of paper.

pleated Having many folds of cloth.

propitious Lucky or favourable.

sarcophagus A large stone box in which a coffin was placed.

smallpox A usually fatal viral infection, spread through the air. Victims suffer fever, chills and aches, followed by itchy, pus-filled red spots.

snare Trap.

stele A piece of stone with writing on it.

stylized Not realistic; following a particular artistic "look".

tuberculosis A usually fatal bacterial infection of the lungs, or the bones and joints.

Two Lands Upper Egypt (the south of the country) and Lower Egypt (the north, where the Nile emptied out into the Mediterranean Sea). Originally two different kingdoms, the Two Lands were united by the pharaoh Menes in around 2900 BCE.

vertebrae Sections of backbone.

Page numbers in **bold** refer to illustrations.